WORD SEARCH PUZZLES
for the WEEKEND

L	Y	E	E	O	R	K	N	U
L	T	I	N	Y	N	U	O	J
O	Y	T	U	A	O	S	Z	O
T	M	F	E	W	T	I	L	S
Y	S	E	X	E	H	W	O	N
A	L	L	I	N	G	R	O	C
P	D	E	T	O	I	S	H	R
A	W	G	N	O	R	W	C	O
U	E	R	R	A	O	O	S	E

ERIC BERLIN

JUNIOR

PUZZLE
WRIGHT
JUNIOR

JUNIOR   New York

An Imprint of Sterling Publishing Co., Inc.
1166 Avenue of the Americas
New York, NY 10036

ISBN 978-1-4549-3165-2

Distributed in Canada by Sterling Publishing, Co., Inc.
c/o Canadian Manda Group, 664 Annette Street
Toronto, Ontario, Canada M6S 2C8
Distributed in the United Kingdom by GMC Distribution Services
Castle Place, 166 High Street, Lewes, East Sussex, England BN7 1XU
Distributed in Australia by NewSouth Books,
University of New South Wales, Sydney, NSW 2052, Australia

For information about custom editions, special sales, and premium and
corporate purchases, please contact Sterling Special Sales at 800-805-5489
or specialsales@sterlingpublishing.com.

Manufactured in Canada
Lot #:
2 4 6 8 10 9 7 5 3 1
11/18

sterlingpublishing.com
puzzlewright.com

CONTENTS

INTRODUCTION

THE FIRST PUZZLE I EVER SOLVED was a word search.

I was very young—maybe four years old. My grandmother brought over a giant book of word searches, and we solved them together sitting side by side on the living room sofa.

I was hooked at once. At first glance, the letters in a word search puzzle are just a meaningless jumble. But you look and you look and eventually—aha! Right there! One of the words in the list jumps out at you, and you proudly get to circle it.

This is the heart and soul of what makes puzzles so much fun. Every puzzle starts off looking like nonsense. With a little applied brainpower, however, you'll soon have an "Aha Moment": You've taken that nonsense and made it make sense. You've solved a crossword clue, or figured out where to place the next sudoku number, or found another word in the word search. Every Aha Moment lights up your brain. It's a wonderfully satisfying feeling. It's the feeling that turned me into a lifelong lover of puzzles. Maybe it will do the same for you, too.

So let's talk about word search puzzles!

Here's how they work: I'll give you a grid of letters. In that grid are hidden a whole bunch of words and phrases, all connected by the puzzle's theme. Your job is to find every one of those words or phrases. Each can be found in a straight line, reading up, down, left, right, or diagonally. When you find one, circle it in the grid. Entries will criss-cross and overlap each other in the grid, so in the completed puzzle, certain letters will be circled more than once.

That's the basics of it, and part of the joy of the word search is that it's such a simple puzzle to understand: Look for a word, find the word, circle the word. But every once in a while, I'm going to throw you a curveball.

- In "Put It Together" (page 21), I've chopped up the word list into tiny pieces. The short words shown in the list can be put together to form longer words; it's these longer words that you'll need to find in the grid. For example, if the words MAN and AGE were in the word list, you would put them together to create the word MANAGE. You'd then try to find MANAGE in the puzzle.

- In "Guess the Theme" (page 34), you get no word list at all! It's up to you to find all 23 entries in the word search grid, and then figure out what those words and phrases have in common.

- "For Short" (page 50) and "Spelling Bee" (page 64) both play a little trick on you. In the first, I'll give you a whole bunch of abbreviations. Hidden in the grid are what those abbreviations stand for. And in the other, the word list is made up of the pronunciations of words, like you'd find in a dictionary. (Or, as the puzzle might have it, a /'dik-shə-ˌne-rē/.) Figure out what words are in the grid by saying them out loud, and then find them in the grid—making sure to spell them correctly, of course.

- For any of these puzzles, if you need help knowing what words have been hidden in the puzzle, never fear: You can find complete word lists on pages 66 and 67.

But wait, we're not done with the curveballs just yet. In a few puzzles—"On Your Mark, Get Set ..." (page 16), "And Now ..." (page 40), and "Black and White" (page 55)—you'll find strange symbols in your word search grid. These are rebuses. In each case, a rebus symbol stands for multiple letters. For example, you'll find ampersands (&) all through the "And Now ..." puzzle. Each ampersand represents the letters AND. So the word HUSBAND would be found in the grid as HUSB&. Get it? And in "Double Up" (page 65), double letters in the word list have been shrunk down to single letters in the grid. Don't worry, though. Each of those puzzles will have a short explanation to remind you of what's going on before you get started.

One more thing: After you've finished circling all the words in a word search, don't rush off to the next puzzle. Instead, take a look at all the letters in the grid that you didn't circle. Read in order from left to right, row by row, they'll spell out a secret message related to that puzzle's theme. It might be a fascinating fact, or a joke, or a riddle you can solve. It's a little bonus—a reward for finding all the words!

A word of thanks to my wonderful wife Janinne, who helped me come up with puzzle ideas and word lists—this book would not exist without her.

Good luck, and happy hunting!

—Eric Berlin

LET'S GET STARTED

All the words in this puzzle contain the
first three letters of the alphabet.

```
H E S U A C E B E C O
C N I B A C A P S L E
L O F U N R L L O U Y
I C T E C T H I O B S
F A S O G C B B B S W
B B D O L A I R A O L
A E D R L R C S C D L
R E L C A T S B O A A
E E O C B B A R I C B
C N B P E U E H P R K
Y U O E U S Z C A Z C
M L B E C K W N A A I
B S C A S C C E A P K
A S A Y A H A A S A S
L B T C A C R O B A T
```

ABSENCE	CARIBOU
ACROBAT	CLIF BAR
BACKUP	CLUB SODA
BACON	CUE BALL
BALCONY	CYMBAL
BAR CODE	KICKBALL
BECAUSE	OBSTACLE
BOBCAT	REBECCA
BRANCH	RIB CAGE
CABIN	SPACE BAR
CABOOSE	SUBTRACT

AT THE LIBRARY

```
C  O  P  I  E  R  O  H  T  U  A
A  L  J  U  V  E  N  I  L  E  E
L  M  U  S  I  C  F  I  B  U  R
L  I  E  C  H  A  S  E  D  R  S
N  N  B  I  C  I  H  R  T  S  E
U  T  O  R  R  A  E  N  E  A  V
M  E  L  C  A  V  L  I  S  S  L
B  R  G  U  O  R  V  U  E  S  E
E  N  N  L  D  O  I  C  U  F  H
R  E  I  A  M  A  N  A  A  I  S
L  T  D  T  L  A  G  Y  N  C  K
D  O  A  I  M  T  C  N  H  T  O
I  N  E  O  G  S  A  B  U  I  O
Y  T  R  N  H  E  R  B  O  O  B
O  K  G  O  L  A  T  A  C  N  Y
```

ARCHIVE	JUVENILE
AUTHOR	LATE FEE
BOOKSHELVES	LIBRARIAN
CALL NUMBER	MOVIES
CATALOG	MUSIC
CIRCULATION	OVERDUE
COPIER	READING
FICTION	ROMANCES
GLOBE	SHELVING CART
INTERNET	YOUNG ADULT

BIRDWATCHING

```
E  L  L  U  G  A  E  S  T  R  H
Y  E  K  R  U  T  E  A  E  T  I
S  N  D  Y  B  F  E  V  G  E  F
S  H  U  A  M  A  O  M  I  L  N
O  P  G  B  K  L  I  R  A  N  E
R  D  H  W  P  C  E  M  I  I  G
T  E  G  E  L  O  I  R  O  U  N
A  G  K  H  A  N  S  H  H  G  I
B  D  J  C  G  S  S  U  C  N  L
L  I  S  O  E  U  A  U  I  E  R
A  R  T  N  R  P  C  N  R  P  A
A  T  A  H  T  K  D  T  T  E  T
N  R  T  T  O  H  S  O  S  O  S
C  A  F  O  A  E  N  O  O  U  N
C  P  N  E  K  C  I  H  C  W  E
```

ALBATROSS	OSTRICH
CHICKADEE	PARTRIDGE
CHICKEN	PENGUIN
CRANE	PHEASANT
CUCKOO	PLOVER
EAGLE	SEAGULL
FALCON	STARLING
FLAMINGO	THRUSH
KESTREL	TURKEY
ORIOLE	WOODPECKER

4

PIXAR PICKS

```
T T Y D O O W A L L E
O U H R A N D A L L E
Y L O S S E N D A S G
S A M E P I N S P I N
T X C A D R T C O C O
O S N L O I G O D M B
R W I A G S S O E A G
Y S S I T H C N F T N
E U R S T H G A I E I
R L E O U N K N L R B
F L T D I I I T S I R
S Y S D O L L F G L A
I O N R R R F S U E V
N I O A T S Y H B Y E
F O M E R I D A A R T
```

"A BUG'S LIFE"　　"FINDING NEMO"　　RANDALL
BING BONG　　FLIK　　RILEY
"BRAVE"　　"INSIDE OUT"　　SADNESS
"COCO"　　MARLIN　　SULLY
DOC HUDSON　　MATER　　"TOY STORY"
DORY　　MERIDA　　WALL-E
ELASTIGIRL　　"MONSTERS, INC."　　WOODY

I CAN SEE YOUR FUTURE

```
S  N  G  I  S  O  M  Y  E  E  S
L  I  F  E  L  I  N  E  I  S  I
E  E  E  R  S  I  Z  E  K  X  B
A  R  A  S  T  R  O  L  O  G  Y
P  M  I  S  N  R  D  E  O  D  L
A  R  E  O  A  L  I  D  C  T  L
L  D  O  C  S  S  A  H  E  O  A
M  E  L  P  R  S  C  A  N  T  B
I  E  O  A  H  T  L  R  U  Y  L
S  T  T  O  P  E  R  E  T  Y  A
T  S  D  R  A  C  T  O  R  A  T
R  D  I  V  C  T  T  C  O  H  S
Y  E  E  F  U  T  S  U  F  R  Y
E  S  O  O  T  H  S  A  Y  E  R
T  N  A  Y  O  V  R  I  A  L  C
```

ASTROLOGY	SCRY
CLAIRVOYANT	SEER
CRYSTAL BALL	SIBYL
DESTINY	SIGN
FORTUNE COOKIE	SOOTHSAYER
LIFELINE	STARS
ORACLE	TAROT CARDS
PALMISTRY	TEA LEAVES
PROPHET	ZODIAC

SEEING RED

```
        T  R  A  E  H
     A  S  L  A  S  B  N
  E  S  O  R  I  B  B  O  N
L  Y  L  A  D  Y  B  U  G  U  B
S  S  R  A  M  H  I  I  A  N  R
G  B  R  R  O  O  S  E  W  K  I
R  E  P  P  E  P  I  L  I  H  C
L  U  O  V  O  H  E  P  R  S  K
  A  B  T  R  E  C  P  B  W
     S  Y  E  T  L  A  L
        R  E  E  R  D
           N
           R
           A
           G
```

APPLE	MARS
BARN	RADISH
BRICK	RIBBON
CHERRY	ROSE
CHILI PEPPER	RUBY
GARNET	SALSA
HEART	STOP SIGN
LADYBUG	WAGON

WHAT'S FOR BREAKFAST?

```
P O R R I D G E S F A
O M E L E T N O A R B
P M R E E L B E U I T
T P A N C A K E S E I
A S B S G I A C A D N
R E A E G G U C G E E
T L L O O I B J E G L
R S O A T M E A L G E
U E N G I H N T C S P
G L A E R E C D L O C
O F R C R I H N P O N
Y F G I U C T O E E F
O A R B B R V S E R A
K W F A S E T I U R F
S N W O R B H S A H T
```

BACON	FRUIT	PANCAKES
BAGEL	GRANOLA BAR	POPOVER
BISCUIT	GRITS	POP-TART
BURRITO	HASH BROWNS	PORRIDGE
COLD CEREAL	JUICE	SAUSAGE
FRENCH TOAST	OATMEAL	WAFFLES
FRIED EGGS	OMELET	YOGURT

ON THE RADIO

```
E  V  A  W  W  E  N  W  H  E  L
N  S  B  O  O  C  S  I  D  A  M
E  F  I  E  N  C  A  D  T  O  N
C  O  G  E  B  S  A  E  E  A  Y
S  L  B  C  H  O  M  E  C  L  L
A  K  A  S  A  Y  P  I  H  Y  O
K  K  N  S  V  L  E  S  N  R  C
L  H  D  A  S  E  Y  E  O  T  E
O  P  E  R  A  I  A  P  V  N  D
P  H  L  G  H  Y  C  M  S  U  Y
E  T  G  E  I  A  L  A  B  O  Z
H  E  N  U  P  E  D  S  L  C  O
R  E  I  L  H  S  T  S  U  N  O
T  M  W  B  O  E  O  E  O  A  N
T  H  S  E  P  T  U  G  S  B  A
```

BEBOP	HEAVY METAL
BIG BAND	HIP-HOP
BLUEGRASS	LATIN
CALYPSO	NEW WAVE
CLASSICAL	OPERA
COUNTRY	POLKA
DANCE	REGGAE
DISCO	SOUL
DUBSTEP	SWING
FOLK	TECHNO
GOSPEL	ZYDECO

ON YOUR MARK, GET SET . . .

Each entry in this puzzle contains the word GO, and in the grid, the letters G and O appear together in a single space.

```
(GO)  D   S   L   A   N   (GO)  A   I   D   I
 S    R   T   A   L   O   Z   N   (GO)  R   (GO)
 A    A   E   L   S   (GO)  E   O   A   N   I
 S    (GO)  L   T   R   A   T   A   A   T   N
 I    N   B   O   E   L   A   T   G   Y   (GO)
 N    G   (GO)  A   D   M   I   E   P   B   U
 V    L   A   Y   E   N   T   D   B   W   T
 I    I   M   A   R   I   (GO)  L   D   T   (GO)
(GO)  N   (GO)  A   T   N   E   P   H   (GO)  I
 R    B   T   L   A   D   N   C   G   K   P
 A    A   (GO)  N   Y   I   A   G   D   (GO)  S
 T    W   R   (GO)  H   (GO)  L   D   B   I   T
 E    S   O   (GO)  N   E   D   L   (GO)  E   S
 D    K   F   T   S   O   I   N   E   A   S
 F    L   A   M   I   N   (GO)  Y   L   O   P
```

DIAGONAL	GORGONZOLA
DRAGON	INDIGO
FLAMINGO	INVIGORATED
FORGOT	LAGOON
GOBBLEDYGOOK	MARIGOLD
GOBLETS	NEGOTIATE
GOBLIN	PAGODA
GOGGLES	PENTAGON
GOING OUT	POLYGON
GOLDEN GOOSE	SPIGOT
GONDOLA	TANGO

MATH CLASS

```
W E R O T C A F H N A
C V T K I V S N O D O
I I F A E Q D I E E S
R T S R U E T N R X T
C A A A D I R T R P N
L G R O D E E N O O
E E R D S A T G O N I
L N A E M E E I E T
L A T C M H M R S N A
A E M I A A A T I T U
R N R M T I I C V N Q
A E G A I M D N I A E
P N E L A N J T D O Y
M Y R T E M O E G E O
S T E L B A I R A V R
```

ADDITION	FACTOR
ANGLE	GEOMETRY
AVERAGE	INTEGER
CIRCLE	NEGATIVE
DECIMAL	PARALLEL
DIAMETER	PERIMETER
DIVISION	REMAINDER
EQUATION	SQUARE
ESTIMATE	UNIT
EXPONENT	VARIABLE

LOOK! UP IN THE SKY!

```
O  U  R  R  A  S  L  U  P  R  S
G  S  E  I  I  A  L  E  A  I  X
Y  A  T  R  G  M  I  C  R  G  H
E  T  I  L  L  E  T  A  S  T  C
H  U  P  A  C  L  L  P  V  O  R
S  R  U  E  A  O  S  S  S  M  E
T  N  J  A  P  H  M  M  N  R  T
A  Y  A  S  S  K  I  E  F  E  T
R  O  U  R  R  C  H  T  T  P  A
S  O  S  E  D  A  I  E  L  P  M
H  U  C  U  N  L  M  O  D  I  K
R  T  S  K  E  B  D  R  B  D  R
I  T  R  L  E  L  I  V  E  G  A
O  N  S  A  S  T  E  R  O  I  D
A  L  U  B  E  N  T  A  R  B  S
```

ASTEROID	JUPITER	ROCKET
BIG DIPPER	MARS	SATELLITE
BLACK HOLE	METEOR	SATURN
COMET	NEBULA	SIRIUS
COSMIC DUST	PLEIADES	SPACE
DARK MATTER	POLARIS	STARS
EARTH	PULSAR	VEGA
	RIGEL	

SCOUT'S HONOR

You can earn many different merit badges in the Boy Scouts.

```
T D G N I K A Y A K G
T H O H E R C G E A W
C E E G R Y E R M O R
H I G A C I N E A F P
E L B L T A D N L L I
S R I A P E R E M O H
S N Y N S J R E U G S
G S T I F K R Y Y K N
N I G M F E E R A T E
I N Y A H S E T E E Z
D S V T E T I S R N I
L T A I T N M E U Y T
E E E O G R I R T T I
W P P N B A D O A G C
D I A T S R I F N E S
```

ANIMATION	GOLF
BASKETRY	HOME REPAIRS
CHESS	KAYAKING
CITIZENSHIP	NATURE
CYCLING	PETS
DOG CARE	POTTERY
ENERGY	SKATING
FIRST AID	THEATER
FORESTRY	WEATHER
GAME DESIGN	WELDING

FAIRY TALE THEATER

```
H T O G R E P P I L S
H A E D S E N E E A E
V E N R L Y C Z B L V
O R D S E O N N D L L
P E I Y E U G L I E E
U H A I P L E T E R G
S T M A I E T V E E P
S O R D N P I H A D P
I M E P G R H N C N I
N P M L B E W O A I Y
B E M E E C W S S C E
O T A E A H O I T V V
O S G E U A N O L R O
T A I F T U S P E L L
S T C E Y N E E U Q R
```

BEAST	OGRE
CASTLE	POISON
CINDERELLA	PRINCE
ELVES	PUSS IN BOOTS
GOLD	QUEEN
GRETEL	RAPUNZEL
HANSEL	SLEEPING BEAUTY
LEPRECHAUN	SLIPPER
LOVE	SNOW WHITE
MAGIC	SPELL
MERMAID	STEPMOTHER

PUT IT TOGETHER

The 40 words seen here can be paired up to form 20 longer words, which can then be found in the grid. For the full word list, see page 66.

```
C A D E W O L L A M R
U A P I G E O N S E T
D S T S T A A C T N H
I P T E T E B N A M U
S H E S R I E R T A E
C A P C H P G L A E V
O L R I R A I I F G I
V T A A L M N L D S T
E Y C F E O N F L P A
R Z O R T U I Y A A N
Y N I T K N N O N R R
I C U S A T G T O R E
K B O L P A T R I O T
H A L E D A R A P W L
R Y D R A H C R O D A
```

ADE	CARP	HALT	PIG
AGE	CATER	INNING	PILLAR
ALL	CHARD	ITS	RANT
ALLY	DIG	LIME	RICK
ALTER	DISCO	NATIVE	RIOT
ASP	ENTER	OR	ROW
BEG	EON	OWED	SIZE
BUT	FIN	PAR	SPAR
CAP	FLAG	PAT	TON
CAR	GARB	PET	VERY

NEW YORK, NEW YORK

```
O  H  N  E  O  K  B  F  A  N  E
W  Y  O  O  R  R  K  I  D  C  I
Y  T  T  O  A  R  N  N  Y  S
A  S  A  N  E  P  Y  M  A  P  N
W  K  X  I  O  L  C  A  L  A  S
D  Y  I  R  K  A  S  N  S  R  M
A  S  T  O  K  R  N  H  I  K  U
O  C  O  Q  A  T  M  A  N  A  E
R  R  E  S  U  N  I  T  E  V  S
B  A  G  E  L  E  S  T  T  E  U
T  P  H  E  B  C  E  A  A  N  M
R  E  T  A  E  H  T  N  T  U  I
G  R  A  Y  A  W  B  U  S  E  S
P  E  D  E  S  T  R  I  A  N  S
A  E  S  L  E  H  C  P  P  L  E
```

AIRPORT	MUSEUMS
BAGEL	MUSIC
BROADWAY	PARK AVENUE
BRONX	PEDESTRIANS
BROOKLYN	QUEENS
BUSES	SKYSCRAPER
CENTRAL PARK	STATEN ISLAND
CHELSEA	SUBWAY
HOTELS	TAXI
MANHATTAN	THEATER

WORDS FROM SPANISH

```
S  P  V  I  G  I  L  A  N  T  E
A  E  T  A  L  O  C  O  H  C  A
D  N  O  Y  N  A  C  N  I  D  G
M  O  S  Q  U  I  T  O  U  A  S
H  H  U  S  I  S  L  C  L  T  H
C  E  S  B  O  E  A  L  C  O  E
A  E  N  O  L  R  E  D  A  M  L
O  D  A  N  R  O  T  M  B  A  O
R  E  O  A  N  T  O  A  S  Z  M
K  P  B  N  T  A  R  N  B  A  A
C  M  O  Z  S  G  P  P  O  L  C
O  A  D  A  O  I  K  A  E  P  A
C  T  E  N  L  L  A  N  T  G  U
U  S  G  A  S  L  A  S  A  I  G
G  E  A  R  M  A  D  I  L  L  O
```

ALBATROSS	CHOCOLATE	PATIO
ALLIGATOR	COCKROACH	PLAZA
ARMADILLO	DOUBLOON	SALSA
BARRACUDA	EMBARGO	STAMPEDE
BODEGA	GALLEON	TORNADO
BONANZA	GUACAMOLE	VANILLA
CANYON	MOSQUITO	VIGILANTE

MYTH MAKERS

```
T  N  R  U  T  A  S  S  H  E  D
D  O  G  R  E  E  E  E  K  E  G
I  D  O  P  T  H  E  R  M  E  S
O  I  D  L  I  S  A  E  L  L  L
N  E  I  U  D  V  T  C  E  O  D
Y  S  N  T  O  E  O  N  L  E  M
S  O  N  O  R  K  O  L  U  N  A
U  P  N  T  H  O  O  L  Y  U  N
S  M  P  A  P  P  A  M  J  T  E
U  I  D  S  A  V  E  U  A  P  H
N  E  M  D  R  R  P  S  W  E  T
S  E  R  E  C  I  E  R  R  N  A
R  U  N  U  T  L  E  A  D  E  B
A  I  R  E  A  R  E  S  Y  Z  P
M  Y  R  E  U  S  A  N  A  I  D
```

APHRODITE	HERMES
APOLLO	JUPITER
ARES	KRONOS
ARTEMIS	MARS
ATHENA	MERCURY
CERES	MINERVA
DEMETER	NEPTUNE
DIANA	PERSEPHONE
DIONYSUS	PLUTO
HADES	POSEIDON
HERA	SATURN

CLEANING UP

```
O  T  N  E  G  R  E  T  E  D  S
N  V  T  H  E  E  N  E  S  U  E
E  T  A  T  W  E  I  K  P  S  V
O  P  A  C  G  A  H  C  L  T  O
R  W  G  N  U  E  C  U  U  P  L
E  S  O  C  L  U  A  B  N  A  G
H  P  B  R  O  O  M  E  G  N  X
S  S  Q  U  E  E  G  E  E  A  E
A  N  I  L  I  N  N  T  R  E  T
W  H  S  L  R  S  I  I  S  E  A
H  N  S  E  O  S  H  E  K  X  L
S  T  Y  U  S  P  S  S  T  N  O
I  R  G  U  R  O  A  P  A  O  S
D  D  E  L  I  B  W  N  E  R  S
S  S  L  E  W  O  T  H  S  I  D
```

BASKET	LATEX GLOVES
BROOM	PLUNGER
BRUSH	POLISH
BUCKET	SOAP
DETERGENT	SPONGE
DISH TOWELS	SQUEEGEE
DISHWASHER	TISSUES
DRYER	VACUUM
DUSTPAN	WASHING MACHINE
IRON	WATER

CRAYOLA-MANIA

```
Y E L L O W C R A B Y
O D N S A R G O L D E
A I N A M A N A N A B
S M O A O R C H I D A
U F G D C K E P F R O
N U N A T N E G A M Y
S C I M P A O A R A R
E H M A C N F T F N A
T S A H I N O W T G N
O I L D E N I M A O A
R A F X O A N D L T C
A C K O L W O R M A E
N I N D I G O U D N S
G A I P E S L D Y G E
E L P R U P L A Y O R
```

BANANAMANIA	ORCHID
BLACK	PEACH
CANARY	PINK FLAMINGO
COTTON CANDY	PLUM
DENIM	ROYAL PURPLE
FUCHSIA	SALMON
GOLD	SEPIA
INDIGO	SHADOW
MAGENTA	SUNSET ORANGE
MANGO TANGO	YELLOW

LET'S GO FOR A DRIVE

```
A  L  M  R  E  D  L  U  O  H  S
D  R  A  V  E  L  O  U  B  E  R
N  I  I  N  O  I  T  C  N  U  J
E  R  C  A  E  Y  S  E  T  L  H
D  O  N  R  O  A  D  X  R  G  I
A  F  E  S  T  W  R  I  U  E  G
E  R  A  U  Q  S  O  T  O  K  H
D  T  N  E  C  S  E  R  C  I  W
Y  A  W  T  L  E  B  A  A  P  A
A  Z  D  R  R  U  M  N  N  Y
V  A  S  T  F  P  E  P  R  R  O
E  L  S  M  B  X  O  V  A  U  S
N  P  T  P  O  E  N  T  O  T  T
U  O  O  R  U  E  O  G  O  L  N
E  T  A  T  S  R  E  T  N  I  C
```

AVENUE
BELTWAY
BOULEVARD
CLOVERLEAF
COURT
CRESCENT
DEAD END
DRIVE
EXIT RAMP
EXPRESSWAY
HIGHWAY

INTERSTATE
JUNCTION
LANE
PLAZA
ROAD
ROTARY
SHOULDER
SPUR
SQUARE
STREET
TURNPIKE

WOOF!

```
W I H R R E T N I O P
A T K D E E O G G B U
R E C U P I R O B M L
O E S P L O R A A B I
T B I M C A O R S R I
T H O R A D S W E H E
W A E X N L P N N T N
E Y U O E U A T J A A
I A K H E R A M I K D
L E I N A P S T U I T
E O F M O U A F T T A
R H I O E M H F I A E
R E D S L T L I L E R
W L T A Y K S U H T G
E E D E Y O M A S C R
```

AKITA	POINTER
BASENJI	POODLE
BOXER	PULI
CHIHUAHUA	ROTTWEILER
CORGI	SALUKI
DALMATIAN	SAMOYED
GREAT DANE	SPANIEL
HUSKY	TERRIER
LHASA APSO	WEIMARANER
MALAMUTE	WHIPPET

SEUSS-ISMS

All of these words were made up by Dr. Seuss.

```
K C A N H C S S E G U
S Q L S R A L S O R C
G U U R E E A T A I K
G A F I E D P C T N H
R C F E M Y K S I C W
I K U L Z N O N I H O
C E R R U D E T N L E
K R T R M P Z Y T R B
L O C D B I P P O L O
E O I K L N I T O D E
G N I L E E G G E F P
R M O O Z A G E I D O
A W R T A A N R N T R
S H E Z Y H Z O O O K
S N E E T C H E S X S
```

BIPPOLO	NINK
BLISPER	QUACKEROO
BLOGG	QUIMNEY
CRUNK CAR	SCHNACK
GAFLUPPTED	SKROPE
GAZOOM	SNEETCHES
GEELING	THNEED
GRICKLE GRASS	TRUFFULA
GRINCH	YOTTLE
GROX	ZILLOW
KLOTZ	ZUMBLE ZAY

WELL, BOWL ME OVER

```
        T  R  E  T  T  U  G
     H  E  G  Y  A  E  A  M  E
  H  W  B     H  E  M  K  E  L  R
  O  A  E  U  S  E  K     C  L  F
  L  T  N  E  M  A  N  R  U  O  T
  E  T  R  D     P  I  K  U  R  P
  S  S  T  R  I  K  E  L  F  T  I
  N  G  H  N  O  C  R  R  I  U  T
  I  S  S  O  A  G  A  L  S  O  O
  L  A  N  E  M  P  P  D  T
  H  I  E  S  S  N  G
```

BUMPERS	POCKET
FOUL	ROLL
FRAME	SHOES
GAME	SPARE
GUTTER	SPLIT
HANDICAP	STRIKE
HOLES	TOURNAMENT
LANE	TURKEY
PINS	

AN EVIL PUZZLE

```
S U T C A L A G Y N O
O U O R T C E L E N N
N C H A N T O H N I A
A V S N E K A I L U S
H M D I I U R B P Q E
T R A U H A O E R Y O
U W E G D G I T D E N
A H D N N O U I T L A
N A A E Z E E R F R M
R M E P S S T U P A O
E R E R K V I O L H W
G N L R E C A F O W T
G N A M D N A S A I A
U D N B R A I N I A C
J O K E R E L D D I R
```

BANE	JUGGERNAUT
BRAINIAC	LOKI
CATWOMAN	MAGNETO
DARKSEID	MANDARIN
DEADSHOT	MR. FREEZE
ELECTRO	PENGUIN
GALACTUS	RIDDLER
GREEN GOBLIN	SANDMAN
HARLEY QUINN	THANOS
JOKER	TWO-FACE

WOODEN IT BE NICE?

```
T E H E A I C A C A W
O R N L O G K N I G T
D Y D I S S O O L D U
O O R E P S U M T L N
O I I R V Q A M I N O
W H U G E N T I A R C
D C E S G B E S I C O
E A H O S Y R R E H C
R T O E V E A E A R Y
F S I V S L E P D T P
M I H A D T R O U L R
A P R E P I N U J E E
P S R A C P N U D Z S
L Y E O A R L S T A S
E L T R Y M O E L H D
```

ACACIA	JUNIPER
ALDER	MANGO
APPLE	MAPLE
APRICOT	MYRTLE
CHERRY	PERSIMMON
CHESTNUT	PINE
COCONUT	PISTACHIO
CYPRESS	REDWOOD
ELDERBERRY	SEQUOIA
GINKGO	SPRUCE
HAZEL	SUMAC

CATS ARE EVERYWHERE!

```
P  E  R  U  T  A  C  I  R  A  C
U  W  E  D  E  L  I  C  A  T  E
S  D  R  E  H  C  T  A  C  E  N
T  H  E  L  T  T  A  C  O  O  I
A  P  T  C  R  E  Y  A  I  O  R
C  N  A  R  A  M  A  T  A  C  E
A  A  C  U  L  T  A  W  R  E  H
T  H  T  A  L  C  H  A  V  C  T
H  I  N  A  I  G  F  L  U  A  A
E  N  A  L  P  E  N  K  O  T  C
D  D  P  W  R  U  T  E  R  N  E
R  P  N  O  E  T  L  A  K  A  I
A  T  T  E  T  N  A  T  C  P  R
L  O  U  V  A  C  A  T  I  O  N
S  T  A  C  C  A  T  O  N  D  L
```

APPLICATION	CATNAP
CARICATURE	CATSUP
CATAMARAN	CATTLE
CATAPULT	CATWALK
CATCHER	DECATHLON
CATERER	DELICATE
CATERPILLAR	LOCATE
CATHEDRALS	STACCATO
CATHERINE	VACATION

GUESS THE THEME

We've hidden the list for this puzzle! Can you find all 23 items and figure out what they have in common? For the full word list, see page 66.

```
R  E  G  A  T  E  F  C  V  E  R
O  W  Y  R  E  N  O  U  T  H  K
T  I  I  E  S  T  O  R  E  N  O
A  N  G  K  O  I  R  T  N  T  O
R  D  U  C  L  H  N  A  R  V  B
E  O  M  O  C  I  U  I  E  A  T
G  W  O  L  C  S  S  N  W  S  C
I  S  U  I  T  C  A  S  E  O  E
R  A  T  O  R  D  A  H  O  S  L
F  F  H  E  A  Z  C  K  R  C  T
E  E  H  D  G  Y  I  R  N  I  T
R  D  C  A  O  E  N  P  O  A  O
P  E  N  T  J  O  Y  A  P  N  B
D  L  I  A  M  E  R  E  C  E  L
O  D  R  A  W  E  R  S  S  E  R
```

B ___ _____
    B ___
    B _____
    C _____
    C _____
  C _____ ___
    C _____
        D ___

D _____
E ____
E ___
G ___
L _____
M ____
O ___

R _____
    S ___
    S ____
  S _____
    S _____
  T __ _____
    W _____
    Z _____

IN THE CLASSROOM

```
S  K  C  A  P  K  C  A  B  T  E
S  K  O  O  B  E  T  O  N  D  E
L  L  C  L  O  C  K  Y  R  O  B
U  R  S  A  L  T  A  A  T  R  O
L  S  R  E  T  S  O  P  E  E  L
I  A  O  R  C  B  H  E  S  H  G
G  R  S  O  E  S  M  T  T  C  A
H  H  S  T  E  T  N  U  P  A  R
T  Y  I  A  I  E  U  E  H  E  B
S  H  C  L  D  C  N  P  L  T  A
W  H  S  U  D  C  K  P  M  A  G
I  V  T  C  I  E  A  E  E  O  E
T  S  A  L  L  T  S  O  R  T  C
C  O  S  A  S  F  C  K  L  S  A
H  A  S  C  H  A  I  R  S  S  N
```

ATLAS	NOTEBOOKS
BACKPACKS	PENCILS
CALCULATOR	POSTERS
CHAIRS	SCISSORS
CLOCK	STAPLER
COMPUTER	STICKERS
DESKS	STUDENTS
GARBAGE CAN	TEACHER
GLOBE	THUMBTACKS
LIGHT SWITCH	WHITEBOARD

HALLOWEEN PARTY

```
T  H  E  S  R  E  T  S  N  O  M
C  O  S  T  U  M  E  S  M  C  N
N  R  O  C  Y  D  N  A  C  T  I
A  G  I  P  A  R  T  Y  A  O  K
N  C  S  I  A  R  A  N  U  B  P
W  O  L  U  I  K  E  E  L  E  M
I  S  T  T  P  R  R  C  D  R  U
Z  O  G  E  I  E  T  A  R  I  P
A  O  I  P  L  T  R  V  O  O  E
R  A  M  W  O  E  O  H  N  A  W
D  A  Y  B  U  H  K  B  E  O  T
V  H  O  Q  I  T  C  S  R  R  I
C  R  S  K  S  E  I  T  A  N  O
D  A  T  F  A  I  R  Y  I  R  E
M  A  G  H  O  S  T  S  T  W  S
```

CANDY CORN	PUMPKIN
CAULDRON	ROBOT
COSTUMES	SCARECROW
FAIRY	SKELETON
GHOSTS	SUPERHERO
MASQUERADE	TRICK OR TREAT
MONSTERS	VAMPIRE
OCTOBER	WITCH
PARTY	WIZARD
PIRATE	ZOMBIE

MARIO KART

```
L E N A P H S A D N O
L E T R O P H Y N I S
A R I A N T E N L A U
B T A E R D O S W H B
W K M M P C L A S C R
O A I O P I R I K E E
N O L G C I P N C R L
S D L K A L L P U I G
Y A S P I N N E R F G
R N T A L N P L T A I
E R O A Y E G I O N W
D O N G C A R T G R D
I T E M B O X R R C O
L A V A M P A N A E Y
G G E I H S O Y C B E
```

BARREL	OIL SLICK
CARGO TRUCK	RAMP
CRATE	SNOWBALL
DASH PANEL	SPINNER
FIRE CHAIN	TORNADO
GLIDER	TROPHY
ITEM BOX	WALKING TREE
LAVA	WARP PIPE
MILLSTONE	WIGGLER BUS
OAK TREE	YOSHI EGG

MILITARY INTELLIGENCE

```
E V R E S E R A A R T
M C I D E M Y I O R F
N E E T N A C R U F P
T A C T I C S C I A S
R T I U R C E R R C R
E E E R A S P A R E E
D N S E M F C F E G T
N L R C B H T T A O R
A I Y I U S H L E O A
M S P T S E F C A L U
M T E S A U A T L T Q
O P H I O E E Y G R D
C M E M P N R E A R A
A A A R F O R T L S E
T C O A R E S A B E H
```

AIRCRAFT	MEDIC
ALLY	PARACHUTE
ARMISTICE	PEACE
BASE	RECRUIT
CAMOUFLAGE	RESCUE
CAMP	RESERVE
CANTEEN	STAR
COMMANDER	SUBMARINES
ENLIST	TACTICS
FORT	TREATY
HEADQUARTERS	TRUCE

THIS IS NONSENSE!

```
G A L P I T E V I J O
T U L I E N C H S O B
O N F F S F U F E A M
N S E F O N A U L O U
P O L L A W S D O C J
O W L E H A E G R N O
P Y D S T R L E E H B
P E U M D N P I D A M
Y B P A R T P A L C U
C S S L R E A O O L M
O H I A T S N H F E D
C B Y R T E H E W K I
K S I K Y E B E A N S
S P T E H S I B B U R
E M E Y E N R A L B N
```

APPLESAUCE	BUSHWA	JIVE
BALDERDASH	CLAPTRAP	MALARKEY
BALONEY	CODSWALLOP	MUMBO JUMBO
BEANS	FOLDEROL	PIFFLE
BLARNEY	FOLLY	POPPYCOCK
BOSH	FUDGE	RUBBISH
BUNK	GUFF	TRIPE

AND NOW . . .

Each entry in this puzzle contains the word AND,
and in the grid, AND appears as an ampersand (&).

```
T  I  A  R  O  &  P  F  K  Y  F
H  R  E  &  I  R  O  C  C  E  O
O  U  W  O  U  T  L  &  I  S  H
U  A  N  M  T  T  O  H  T  G  R
S  E  L  T  S  A  C  &  S  &  &
&  S  G  T  &  R  F  O  E  R  T
R  L  Y  R  E  &  M  A  L  A  S
O  O  E  K  &  A  &  U  &  B  R
R  &  &  R  G  M  N  F  C  Y  E
R  H  L  I  I  I  O  &  E  &  D
N  D  C  R  S  Y  I  T  O  C  N
U  W  P  S  O  D  L  H  H  O  U
&  E  U  L  A  D  E  D  O  E  A
R  H  &  T  S  T  &  A  R  D  R
S  T  E  &  H  T  D  I  W  &  B
```

BANDWIDTH
CANDIDATE
CANDLESTICK
CANDY BAR
CORIANDER
DANDELION
GRANDMOTHER
HANDKERCHIEF
IRELAND
MAGIC WAND

ORLANDO
OUTLANDISH
PANDORA
RANDOM
REPRIMAND
SANDCASTLE
SALAMANDER
STANDARD
THOUSAND
UNDERSTAND

BICYCLE RIDE

```
S  P  I  R  G  T  E  K  S  A  B
P  M  U  P  R  I  A  X  L  E  S
O  E  E  B  U  T  R  E  N  N  I
K  D  S  O  M  T  O  E  S  O  H
E  N  E  N  E  E  T  W  D  A  H
S  A  O  M  P  R  C  O  N  M  O
S  T  L  S  A  P  E  D  A  L  S
C  E  T  E  T  R  L  S  T  B  I
H  C  L  Y  C  E  F  L  S  C  E
W  S  I  B  B  B  E  S  K  H  S
I  A  S  A  A  P  R  R  C  R  O
N  K  R  E  S  C  H  A  I  O  P
N  S  E  R  I  T  O  E  K  M  E
E  T  I  H  P  A  R  G  R  E  S
O  A  L  U  M  I  N  U  M  N  S
```

AIR PUMP	GEARS	PEDALS
ALUMINUM	GRAPHITE	REFLECTOR
AXLES	GRIPS	SCHWINN
BASKET	HANDLEBARS	SEAT
BRAKES	HELMET	SPOKES
CABLES	HORN	STEER
CHROME	INNER TUBE	TANDEM
FRAME	KICKSTAND	TIRES

ONLY O

```
R C O K N R O H G O F
O C O W O R R O M O T
O O H M W O S M L O M
D O C H M O B K R O N
T L O S H O S K N K C
N O O S P O N S O R N
O K H G N O O C O O W
R G C G F O W S O W C
F N S L N O S S N L R
H O O M H W T O O O D
T K G W O H O O T O O
O G O R S P R O P H R
T N D S S G M O B C T
K O N W O D W O L S O
O H N R O C P O P O H
```

CHOO-CHOO	HONG KONG	POT OF GOLD
COMMON COLD	HOT ROD	SCHOOLWORK
COOKBOOK	KNOW-HOW	SLOW DOWN
CROSSWORD	MONSOON	SNOWSTORM
FOGHORN	MOTOR	SPONSOR
FOLK SONG	POMPOMS	SPOON
FRONT DOOR	POPCORN	TOMORROW

FABRIC STORE

```
Y  E  N  I  D  R  A  B  A  G  O
C  A  L  I  C  O  O  U  M  N  R
C  E  A  L  N  W  L  E  I  L  G
N  R  N  A  I  R  A  H  N  E  A
I  I  E  I  A  N  C  M  E  A  N
L  D  T  K  L  R  E  O  D  T  D
P  E  S  A  C  O  S  H  A  H  Y
O  T  R  H  S  U  N  A  C  E  O
P  N  U  M  E  Y  S  I  S  R  O
E  N  O  B  G  N  I  R  R  E  H
R  U  L  F  C  A  E  N  E  C  T
C  W  E  E  F  J  A  N  R  E  A
A  H  V  O  M  I  E  A  I  E  S
L  L  I  W  T  D  H  D  R  L  E
E  R  E  M  H  S  A  C  S  F  S
```

CALICO	LACE
CASHMERE	LEATHER
CHENILLE	LINEN
CHIFFON	MOHAIR
CHINO	ORGANDY
CRINOLINE	PERCALE
DENIM	POPLIN
FLEECE	SATIN
GABARDINE	SEERSUCKER
HERRINGBONE	TWILL
JERSEY	VELOUR

BRRR!

```
        S  E  E
     V  T  C  E  R
     Y  O  E  R  S
     O  E  E
  S  B  L  T  L
N  O  N  F  A  L  S
W  F  F  O  E  L  A
I  K  R  N  W  H  E
C  N  O  S  M
P  A  I  U  S  I  A
H  L  A  L  C  S  T  S  N
F  O  S  A  I  L  T  D  X
S  W  R  I  D  D  E  L  S
E  F  R  O  Z  E  N  O  S
L  E  V  O  H  S  C
```

BOOTS	PLOW
COLD	SCARF
FLANNEL	SHOVEL
FLEECE	SLED
FROST	SLEET
FROZEN	SLUSH
ICICLE	SNOWMAN
MITTENS	SWEATER

AROUND THE WORLD

```
W A C H A I T A P T C
R I O H N A S U O E N
A L T R I Y C R L C D
C O O W T N N T A E N
S G A A N I A I N E A
A N A N E N L S D R L
G O I T G A E A H G I
A M R E R P H D C D Z
D O T T A C A N E S A
A I S E N O D N I W W
M U U I E L M C A U S
A T A I A A V E F M L
E P T P R U S S I A A
S Y E K R U T T J E R
S N F G B R A Z I L H
```

ARGENTINA	MADAGASCAR
AUSTRALIA	MONGOLIA
AUSTRIA	NEPAL
BRAZIL	PANAMA
CHAD	POLAND
CHINA	RUSSIA
DENMARK	SPAIN
FIJI	SWAZILAND
GREECE	SWEDEN
INDONESIA	TAIWAN
ISRAEL	TURKEY

ICE CREAM PARLOR

```
W O L L A M H S R A M
A L L I N A V I S I C
S U N D A E R E L A M
Y Y D A O R Y K C O R
R C P O O C S M I O S
R A U S S D C H I R O
E R E A H N C M W N F
B A N A N A S P L I T
W M E A T S K L L T S
A E S S C E R E E O E
R L I E F I A B M P R
T P F U O K R C R P V
S I D T A O L F O I E
C G E C S O R E A N M
E T A L O C O H C G E
```

BANANA SPLIT
CARAMEL
CHOCOLATE
CONE
COOKIES AND CREAM
FLOAT
FUDGE
MARSHMALLOW
MILK
MINT

PISTACHIO
ROCKY ROAD
SCOOP
SHAKE
SOFT SERVE
SORBET
STRAWBERRY
SUNDAE
TOPPING
VANILLA

GIDDY-UP!

```
W  P  D  H  B  R  I  D  L  E  A
P  E  L  D  D  A  S  E  D  I  S
O  D  A  S  N  I  E  R  T  E  S
L  I  B  O  S  Y  E  B  O  B  E
L  G  E  L  N  P  A  H  C  D  N
A  R  I  O  M  I  S  G  H  R  R
G  E  P  U  K  E  M  U  A  E  A
N  E  J  C  S  N  S  O  G  S  H
I  D  W  R  H  B  H  R  L  S  I
L  T  O  E  A  E  O  O  A  A  N
R  H  D  N  E  O  S  H  A  G  P
A  T  D  S  M  L  I  T  K  E  E
E  R  A  I  H  W  H  I  N  N  Y
Y  O  N  R  G  N  A  T  S  U  M
S  G  E  G  N  I  N  I  A  R  T
```

BRIDLE	PALOMINO
CHESTNUT	PEDIGREE
DRESSAGE	PIEBALD
GALLOP	PONY
GROOMING	REINS
HARNESS	SIDESADDLE
HORSESHOES	THOROUGHBRED
HUSBANDRY	TRAINING
JUMPER	WHINNY
MUSTANG	YEARLING

FANCY FOOTWORK

```
S P M U P
E K W H M
O A I U T
H S L S K
S E A I N
S D S N D
F A R N D
L L O O I A
A B I F F S L
T R M P S X A S U
S E S G P S O C K S
I L O A F E R S C T C
D L O         R S H O O
C O E         S S O M
L R I         K B E
```

BOOTS	OXFORDS
CLOGS	PUMPS
FLATS	ROLLERBLADES
FLIPPERS	SANDALS
LOAFERS	SHOES
MOCCASINS	SKIS
MULES	SOCKS

TRAVELING MONEY

```
T H S E A R I P M E L
M I H Q N T M I N A E
H A I P U R U T A Y K
U S L T R E R U B L E
A L L I G A T O O N H
A C I Y T O L Z C E S
Y N N C R I U E A A T
I A G E V D G R A L C
U R O I A U N G D T M
G F A K I A E G N E T
U N I L W N Y I T I T
O H D A L A R I T W R
E E I G H O C S F O V
R E R O F A D H N U E
T A O B L A B O A N R
```

BALBOA (Panama)	NGULTRUM (Bhutan)
BOLIVIANO (Bolivia)	OUGUIYA (Mauritania)
DOLLAR (United States)	QUETZAL (Guatemala)
FORINT (Hungary)	RINGGIT (Malaysia)
FRANC (Switzerland)	RUBLE (Russia)
GOURDE (Haiti)	RUFIYAA (The Maldives)
GUILDER (The Netherlands)	RUPIAH (Indonesia)
KWACHA (Zambia)	SHEKEL (Israel)
KYAT (Myanmar)	SHILLING (England)
LEMPIRA (Honduras)	TENGE (Kazakhstan)
METICAL (Mozambique)	ZLOTY (Poland)

FOR SHORT

The twenty words in this puzzle are not shown—instead, we're providing you with each entry's abbreviation. Can you figure out what each abbreviation means and find it in the grid? The full word list can be found on page 67.

```
W G H T E E R T S A F
T E C I G M R T Y L A
S N N N D A S M U T C
U E O A U R L I T E E
I R I Q H G D L A R N
S A T V E O T E O O T
L L A R U L P S O N I
E H I N E I S P A R M
C T C M L K S E A E E
A E O E A E B R K V T
P X S D L B N H S O E
T A S B N H R O A G R
A S A E C U V U L I A
I T T N I O O R A O N
N O I T A R O P R O C
```

AK	Gov.
assn.	in.
C	kg
Capt.	lb.
cm	mph
Col.	pl.
corp.	qt.
fl. oz.	st.
gal.	tbsp.
Gen.	TX

TOY STORE

```
E  Y  S  A  E  S  L  I  N  K  Y
S  T  K  C  I  K  K  A  R  O  D
L  T  C  B  B  C  O  C  E  G  A
E  U  A  H  R  I  R  L  O  E  P
E  P  J  M  A  T  T  E  L  L  D
H  Y  B  B  B  S  O  X  A  A  B
W  L  N  D  I  O  K  Y  A  S  T
T  L  I  H  C  G  D  E  N  K  A
O  I  W  R  I  O  W  U  T  E  B
H  S  K  J  H  P  G  H  O  C  C
T  H  O  L  I  R  U  N  E  T  H
H  E  E  T  E  O  Y  Z  H  E  A
A  L  L  T  O  D  F  F  Z  A  L
O  N  A  I  P  Y  O  T  M  L  K
E  W  E  P  O  R  P  M  U  J  E
```

BARBIE	MATTEL
BIG WHEEL	MODEL KIT
BLOCKS	PLAY-DOH
CHALK	POGO STICK
ETCH-A-SKETCH	PUZZLE
G.I. JOE	SILLY PUTTY
HOT WHEELS	SLINKY
JACKS	TOY PIANO
JUMP ROPE	WATER GUN
LEGO	WHISTLE

ELEMENTARY

```
H I C N S S M A A L Y
E C N N O U N E W E R
L T O D I B N O K K U
I H I N N Z R R R C C
U U A N O O Y A O I R
M R P E E P C B C N E
U D P G T T A I O P M
N O R O B L N L L E U
I A N R T E E A R I I
M R N D G A T H E O S
U W T Y O I S T V U E
L U X H N R G S L N N
A O L U E A N F I D G
I N M T O G U O S U A
L N E G O R T I N D M
```

ALUMINUM	NITROGEN
BORON	OXYGEN
CARBON	PLATINUM
COBALT	POTASSIUM
HELIUM	SILICON
HYDROGEN	SILVER
IRON	SODIUM
KRYPTON	SULFUR
MAGNESIUM	TUNGSTEN
MERCURY	URANIUM
NICKEL	ZINC

CLIMB EVERY MOUNTAIN

```
N O T G N I H S A W T
T S E R E V E H S E K
V N E R Y D B E N C K
B O S T A L P S A M A
M W O C D H U P I N E
I T S A I D O O H E P
L A I K R N C L C G S
C I E M O B E A A D E
O R A J N A M I L I K
R E E S D P T R A R I
E I E I A E Y T P E P
O N P S C T N A P U Y
I I O N K A P A A L E
A A R T S K L C L B O
N R D I S T I G O I N
```

ADIRONDACKS	HIKE
ALPS	HOOD
APPALACHIANS	KILIMANJARO
BLUE RIDGE	PACK
CAMP	PIKES PEAK
CASCADES	RAINIER
CLIMB	ROPE
DENALI	SNOW
EVEREST	STONE
GLACIER	WASHINGTON

A GOLD MEDAL PUZZLE

```
G A Y R E H C R A T E
N N S N O W B O A R D
I Y S C E A V R G E O
L L K N D B O O N Y L
C E A O O W L I I O L
Y Q T T N T L A X M A
C U I N E O E F O T B
D E N I P A Y L B A T
L S G M A T B O E E E
T T A D H E A G F K K
T R I A T H L O N W S
T I I B L R L J S O A
T A O R U G B Y U N B
L N Y M G N I V I D P
S I N N E T I C S O O
```

ARCHERY	LUGE
BADMINTON	RUGBY
BASKETBALL	SKATING
BOXING	SKELETON
CYCLING	SNOWBOARD
DIVING	TAE KWON DO
EQUESTRIAN	TENNIS
GOLF	TRAMPOLINE
HOCKEY	TRIATHLON
JUDO	VOLLEYBALL

BLACK AND WHITE

Each entry in this puzzle contains BLACK and/or WHITE. In the grid, BLACK appears as a dark square, and WHITE as a light square.

```
R ☐ A S A S H E E T A
R E H T N A P ■ I C C
M E N I N ■ H O L E ■
O I D O ■ N S S ☐ T C
A K ☐ ☐ R B A N E O A
N O B L A Y E J L S D
■ O L E S N P L T E O
K C O ☐ P I D N T ☐ S
N ☐ O W B ■ E B I H Y
I D D O E R Y ☐ L O R
G N C N R A E N D U R
H A E S R S ■ A H S E
T ■ L A Y D E S D E H
O F L F G ■ M A G I C
R A S Y ☐ B O A R D ■
```

BLACK AND WHITE COOKIE
BLACK BELT
BLACK CHERRY SODA
BLACK-EYED PEAS
BLACK HOLE
BLACK KNIGHT
BLACK MAGIC
BLACK PANTHER
BLACK RASPBERRY
JET BLACK

LITTLE WHITE LIE
MEN IN BLACK
RED, WHITE, AND BLUE
SNOW WHITE
WHITE AS A SHEET
WHITE BLOOD CELLS
WHITEBOARD
WHITE BREAD
WHITE FLAG
WHITE HOUSE

"S" ANIMALS

```
        S K R A H S O
      M S N A W S H E G
    E S Q U I R R E L A S
    R N U K A     E K T L
    E E I S S     P S S L
      I D H P
      T N S O H
        E A I N R
        S M F G N
          A R E E
  T S A K     I L A L H
  Y A K S     I O A T U
  T N O I L A E S O S S
  H W T N O M L A S
      A S S K S R D
```

SALAMANDER	SNAIL
SALMON	SPONGE
SEAL	SQUID
SEA LION	SQUIRREL
SHARK	STAG
SHEEP	STARFISH
SKINK	STOAT
SKUNK	SWAN
SLOTH	

AT THE GAME

```
T  H  S  E  T  E  L  H  T  A  E
A  S  M  U  T  S  R  S  O  D  D
O  L  R  M  N  E  T  I  O  N  P
H  F  O  A  O  N  R  M  U  R  S
S  T  F  C  A  M  E  R  A  S  O
N  E  I  N  K  A  F  T  T  E  S
X  G  N  I  R  E  E  H  C  C  E
P  E  U  I  A  T  R  S  O  V  Q
P  O  W  A  L  O  E  R  A  S  U
S  T  P  H  E  G  E  W  O  G  I
C  F  I  C  R  B  E  S  T  O  P
D  I  O  S  O  H  C  A  N  D  M
M  E  D  A  T  R  D  S  T  T  E
A  D  R  E  G  A  N  A  M  O  N
I  D  U  M  M  C  O  A  C  H  T
```

ATHLETES	MANAGER
CAMERAS	MEDIC
CHEERING	NACHOS
COACH	PENNANTS
DOME	POPCORN
EQUIPMENT	REFEREE
FANS	SCOREBOARD
"GO TEAM!"	TARP
HOT DOGS	THE WAVE
LINES	TURF
LOCKER ROOM	UNIFORMS

THANK Q

```
H T O X O N I U Q E W
E E N S Q U I D E Q U
T U I I C T I U K L Y
T Q U L I U Q N A R T
E N Q C Q R A N P Y O
U A E I A Q U N H A M
Q B L M M U E M Y A S
I T R H P O U E S N E
T A A M E I R Q I I U
E C H A R S U U Q N Q
C Q I A T E Q Q U Y I
T H U F R E Q U E N T
A Q T A S H A S A T N
A W D S L E U Q E S A
O E E U Q S O M Q S H
```

ANTIQUE	MARQUEE
AQUARIUM	MASQUERADE
BANQUET	MOSQUE
EQUALS	PHYSIQUE
EQUINOX	SEQUELS
EQUIPMENT	SEQUINS
ETIQUETTE	SQUASH
FREQUENT	SQUID
HARLEQUIN	TRANQUIL
LIQUID	TURQUOISE

IN THE KITCHEN

```
E G N O P S I N K W E
L W O B R A G U S L H
T A R T T R W O D F S
T M I C R O W A V E G
E R E U E T L I T A N
K T L S M A A R R I O
S E F E I R A B P R T
I A F R T E A G N E E
H S A A Y G N G S N L
W P W K E I E R E E L
A O R C L R N F C P I
M O A L S F N G I O K
F N O O F E E A P N S
C R H O V R T H S A K
E R K O O B K O O C N
```

CAN OPENER	ROLLING PIN
COOKBOOK	SINK
FORK	SKILLET
FRYING PAN	SPICES
GARBAGE CAN	SPONGE
KETTLE	SUGAR BOWL
KNIFE	TEASPOON
LADLE	TIMER
MICROWAVE	TONGS
OVEN	WAFFLE IRON
REFRIGERATOR	WHISK

SPELLING BEE

The words in this puzzle are not shown—instead, we're
providing you with each one's pronunciation from the dictionary.
Can you figure out how each word is spelled and find it in the grid?
The complete word list is on page 67.

```
N  P  E  D  E  F  I  N  I  T  E
V  R  E  O  R  T  T  E  M  N  R
L  O  L  U  H  W  I  I  T  A  E
R  C  C  G  H  E  N  S  D  E  V
O  E  I  H  T  I  H  N  A  G  U
B  E  S  T  A  T  E  S  F  R  E
H  D  H  T  E  L  Y  S  O  E  N
G  S  U  P  A  E  W  A  R  S  A
I  R  A  C  Q  U  I  R  E  L  M
E  L  H  E  D  H  R  R  I  S  S
N  O  M  Y  E  O  T  A  G  S  U
C  O  L  U  M  N  H  B  N  I  T
N  N  G  I  S  E  D  M  G  T  C
W  R  E  R  U  S  I  E  L  O  A
Y  R  O  G  E  T  A  C  N  G  C
```

'ä-nəst	im-'ber-əs	'mi-nē-ə-ˌchər
'de-fə-nit	'kak-təs	'nā-bər
di-'zīn	'käl-əm	prə-'sēd
dō	'kal-ən-dər	're-stə-ˌränt
ə-'kwir	'ka-tə-ˌgôr-ē	rīm
'fôr-ən	'lē-zhər	rist
hīt	mə-'nü-vər	'sär-jənt

DOUBLE UP

Each entry in this puzzle has at least two pairs of double letters.
In each case, the double letters appear in the grid
combined into a single letter.

```
H  A  A  L  E  R  A  Z  O  M  P
T  E  N  I  S  B  A  L  I  N  B
N  S  E  W  E  S  I  S  E  O  U
F  I  N  R  N  F  D  W  K  B  L
E  I  N  O  G  T  O  E  H  A  E
L  E  T  P  Z  L  P  C  S  K  T
Z  E  O  I  A  E  E  E  N  E  P
A  C  H  H  R  R  B  E  R  P  R
D  E  S  W  F  T  D  U  O  M  O
E  E  F  L  S  E  D  S  T  G  F
L  T  O  A  P  I  E  G  A  O  E
Z  T  A  I  N  A  R  W  T  D  N
A  O  R  M  D  S  U  E  E  E  A
R  Y  A  D  O  G  C  R  F  S  C
H  P  U  E  G  R  O  L  Z  L  E
```

BOOKKEEPER	OCCURRED
BULLETPROOF	OFFSHOOT
COFFEE	PEEK-A-BOO
EGGROLL	RAZZLE-DAZZLE
FERRIS WHEEL	ROOMMATE
GODDESS	SNOOZE BUTTON
GOOD DAY	TATTOO
HALLOWEEN	TENNIS BALL
KNEE-DEEP	TOLL-FREE
MOZZARELLA	WHIPPOORWILL

HONEST	EMBARRASS	MINIATURE
DEFINITE	CACTUS	NEIGHBOR
DESIGN	COLUMN	PROCEED
DOUGH	CALENDAR	RESTAURANT
ACQUIRE	CATEGORY	RHYME
FOREIGN	LEISURE	WRIST
HEIGHT	MANEUVER	SERGEANT

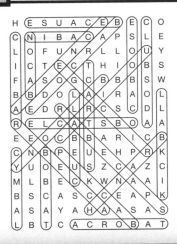

14 PUT IT TOGETHER

ALLOWED	DISCOVERY
ALTERNATIVE	FINALLY
ASPHALT	FLAGRANT
BEGINNING	GARBAGE
BUTTON	LIMERICK
CAPSIZE	ORCHARD
CARPENTER	PARADE
CARPET	PATRIOT

·ANSWERS·

1 LET'S GET STARTED

Hopefully this word search puzzle was as easy as ABC.

2 AT THE LIBRARY

Librarians usually do things by the book.

3 BIRDWATCHING

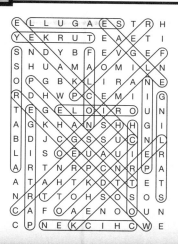

The tiny bee hummingbird weighs just a tenth of an ounce.

4 PIXAR PICKS

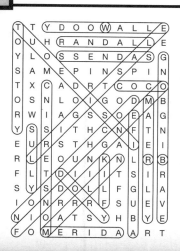

The lamp in Pixar's logo was the star of its first short.

9 ON YOUR MARK, GET SET...

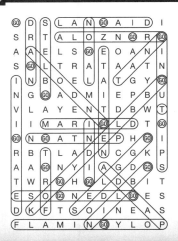

Go is also a strategy game played with black and white stones.

10 MATH CLASS

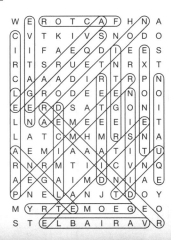

What kind of a dessert does a mathematician enjoy most? (Pi)

11 LOOK! UP IN THE SKY!

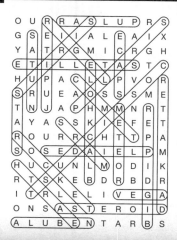

Our galaxy might have as many as four hundred billion stars.

12 SCOUT'S HONOR

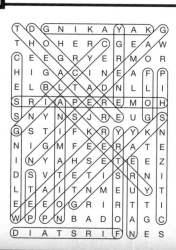

There were originally just fifty-seven merit badges.

13 — FAIRY TALE THEATER

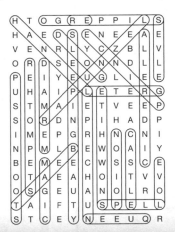

Then everybody lived happily ever after.

14 — PUT IT TOGETHER

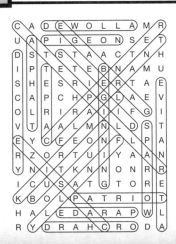

A mustache must ache if you yank on it too hard.

15 NEW YORK, NEW YORK

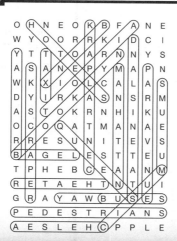

One of New York City's nicknames is the Big Apple.

16 WORDS FROM SPANISH

Spanish is the second-most-spoken language.* (*behind Chinese)

17 MYTH MAKERS

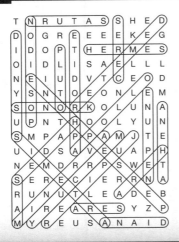

The Greek Gods all lived on Mount Olympus and were ruled by Zeus.

18 CLEANING UP

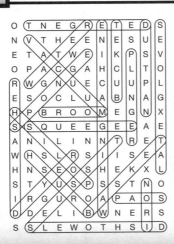

On these two pages, cleanliness is next to godliness.

19 CRAYOLA-MANIA

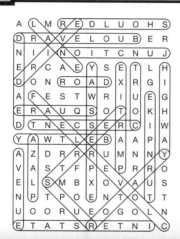

Crayons are made from paraffin wax and colored dye.

20 LET'S GO FOR A DRIVE

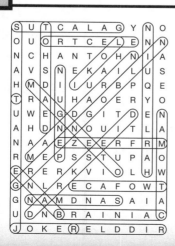

America's longest road runs from Boston to Oregon.

24 AN EVIL PUZZLE

You can't have a superhero without a supervillain.

21 · WOOF!

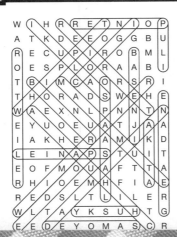

What dog becomes a bird when you take off the first letter? ("Beagle" becomes "eagle.")

25 · WOODEN IT BE NICE?

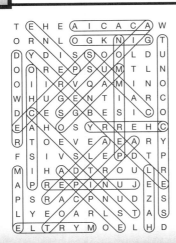

The world's oldest living tree is over five thousand years old.

26 · CATS ARE EVERYWHERE!

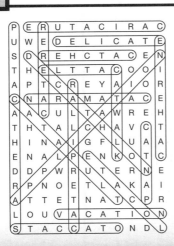

We hope you're having fun and we're not kitten around.

27 GUESS THE THEME

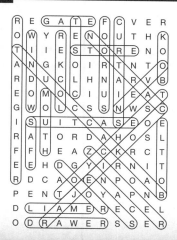

Everything in this word search grid can open and close.

28 IN THE CLASSROOM

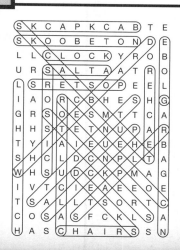

Tell your teachers they have a lot of class.

29 | HALLOWEEN PARTY

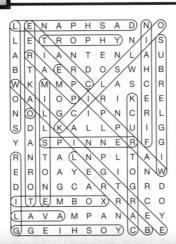

The magician likes to give away both tricks and treats.

30 | MARIO KART

Nintendo was originally a playing card company.

31 MILITARY INTELLIGENCE

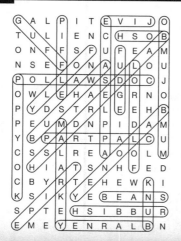

Army officers prefer to shop at the general store.

32 THIS IS NONSENSE!

A little nonsense now and then is relished by the wisest men.

33 AND NOW ...

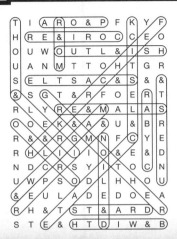

If you want to
grandstand
for your friends,
you should do
a handstand.

34 BICYCLE RIDE

Someone who
promotes
bicycles is a
spokes-person.

35 ONLY O

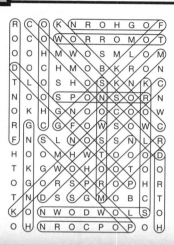

Cows moo.
Horns honk.
Owls hoot.
Ghosts go boo.

36 FABRIC STORE

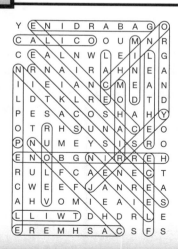

You can wear a
dress at home.
You can't wear
a home address.

37 BRRR!

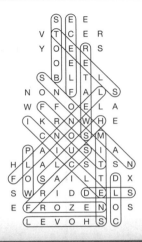

Every snowflake has six sides.

38 AROUND THE WORLD

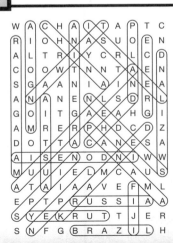

What country contains the consecutive letters F G H? (Afghanistan)

39 | ICE CREAM PARLOR

I scream,
you scream,
we all scream
for ice cream.

40 | GIDDY-UP!

What's black
and white
and eats like
a horse?
(A zebra)

41 FANCY FOOTWORK

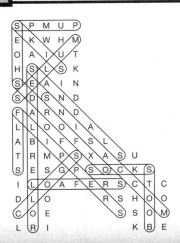

What kind of music do shoes like? (Sole music)

42 TRAVELING MONEY

The mint in Australia once created a coin that weighs over one ton.

43 FOR SHORT

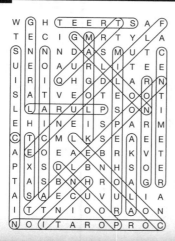

What city and state have the same abbreviation? (LA: Los Angeles and Louisiana)

44 TOY STORE

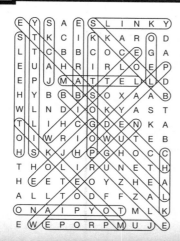

A cardboard box and a stick are both in the Toy Hall of Fame.

45 ELEMENTARY

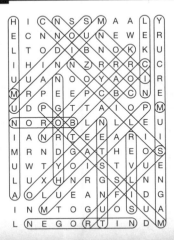

Isaac Newton hoped to learn how to turn lead into gold.

46 CLIMB EVERY MOUNTAIN

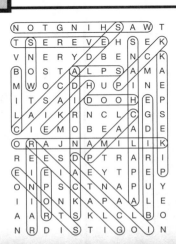

The very best mountain climbers try to stay in peak condition.

47 — A GOLD MEDAL PUZZLE

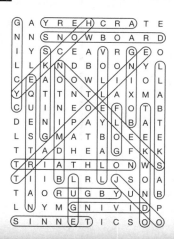

A ten-year-old boy won a medal at the first Olympics.

48 — BLACK AND WHITE

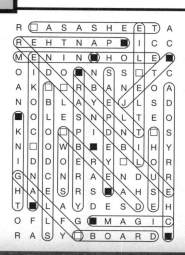

Raccoons can only see in black, white, and shades of gray.

49 | "S" ANIMALS

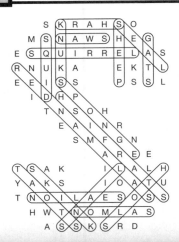

Some snakes slither sneakily southward.

50 | AT THE GAME

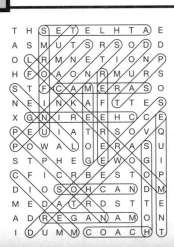

The Astrodome in Houston, Texas, was the first domed stadium.

51 THANK Q

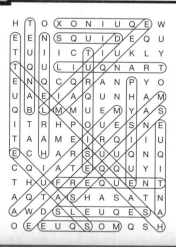

How quickly can you name the American city that has two Qs? (Albuquerque)

52 GOTTA CATCH 'EM ALL

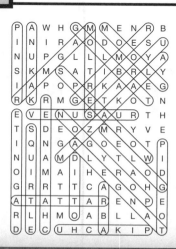

When birds play Pokémon, they've gotta hatch 'em all.

53 FLOUR POWER

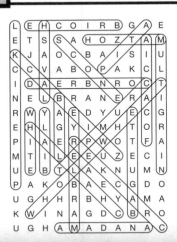

Get a job as a baker and you can make dough by making dough.

54 NAME GAME

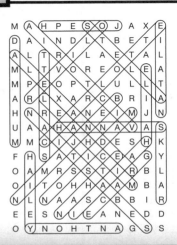

Max and Bella are popular names for both babies and dogs.

55   X-RAY VISION

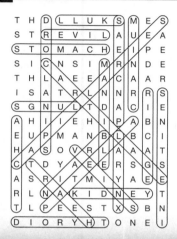

The stapes,
inside the ear,
is the human
body's smallest
bone.

56   IN THE KITCHEN

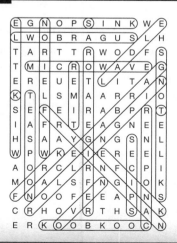

What two fruits
are anagrams
of each other?
(LEMON and
MELON)

57 SPELLING BEE

```
N P E D E F I N I T E
V R E O R T T E M N R
L O L U H W I T A E V
R C C G H E N S D E U
O E I H T I H N A G E
B E S T A T E S F R N
H D H T E L Y S O R A
G S U P A E W A R L M
I R A C Q U I R E L S
E L H E D H R R I S U
N O M Y E O T A G S T
C O L U M N H B N I T
N N G I S E D M G T C
W R E R U S I E L O A
Y R O G E T A C N G C
```

Never tell witches that they spelled something wrong.

58 DOUBLE UP

```
H A A L E R A Z O M P
T E N I S B A L I N B
N S E W E S I S E O U
F I N R N F D W K B L
E I N O G T O E H A E
L E T P Z L P C S K T
Z E O I A E E E N E P
A C H H R R B E R P R
D E S W F T D U O M O
E E F L S E D S T G F
L T O A P I E G A O E
Z A T A I N A R W T D N
A O R M D S U E E E A
R Y A D O G C R F S C
H P U E G R O L Z L E
```

Happiness is finding the secret message in a word search puzzle.